PROPERTY OF
ST. CLEMENT'S
LIBRARY
ROSEDALE, MD.

SUN · SIGN

SUN · SIGN

CANCER
by paula taylor

creative education
childrens press

S U N · S I G N

Published by Creative Education, Inc., 123 South Broad Street, Mankato, Minnesota 56001 Copyright © 1978 by Creative Education, Inc. International copyrights reserved in all countries. No part of this book may be reproduced in any form without written permission from the publisher. Printed in the United States.

Library of Congress Cataloging in Publication Data

Taylor, Paula.
  Cancer.

  SUMMARY: Describes character traits and attitudes reputedly possessed by individuals born under the sun sign Cancer.
  1. Cancer (Astrology)—Juvenile literature.
[1. Cancer (Astrology) 2. Astrology] I. Title.
BF1727.3.T39   133.5'2   77-12676
ISBN 0-87191-644-4

SUN · SIGN

CANCER
contents

Your sun sign is cancer	7
But you're probably not 100% cancer	14
Your cancerian appearance	17
What you might expect — if your sun sign is cancer	19
School	19
Sports and hobbies	26
Money	28
New Things	31
Travel	33
Home and family	34
Friends	36
Health Rx for cancer	37
Other cancerians like you	39
If your older sister is a cancerian	39
If your mother is a cancerian	41
If your grandfather is a cancerian	42
Cancerian careers	44
Famous people born under the sign of cancer	46

C A N C E R

your sun sign is cancer

If your birthday is between
June 21 and July 23
Your sun sign is Cancer.
Your key word is "I feel."
Your ruler is the Moon.
Your element is water.
Your symbol is the Crab.
Your energy is cardinal.
Your color is pale gold.
Your metal is silver.
Your flower is the lily.
Your stone is the pearl, or moonstone.

Have you ever watched a crab
skittering along the sand
with its comical sideways gait?
If your sun sign is Cancer,
you should observe the crab carefully,
for his ways are very like your own.

C   A   N   C   E   R

Dangle something shiny in front of a crab.
He won't be able to resist such a treasure.
But he probably won't grab it right away.
He'll hang back cautiously and watch it for a
    while.
He'll sidle up to it—then back away.
You'll think he's lost interest.
But if you start moving the object away from
    him,
he'll lunge forward and grab it.
Once he's got his treasure,
he'll never relinquish it.
He'll lose a claw rather than let go.

If your sun sign is Cancer
you are as cautious and tenacious as the
    crab.
Before you go after something
you will carefully calculate the risks.
You will seem to be moving in every
    direction
except straight ahead.
But in the end you will make your move
quickly and decisively.
Most likely you will get what you want.

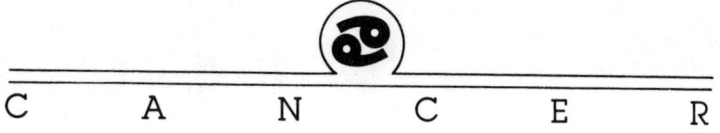

C A N C E R

And once you've got it, you won't let go.
You will cling firmly
to friends, family and possessions,
and you will go to great lengths
to protect them from harm.

Like the crab who remains motionless for hours
under a rock,
you can spend time by yourself
and not feel lonesome.
You don't like meeting new people,
for you are uneasy in the presence of strangers.
You relax only in the company of those
you trust completely.
Like the crab, you have a hard outer shell.
Those who don't know you
may find you cold and aloof.
When threatened,
you may be short-tempered and snappish.
But you wear your hard shell for protection.
as the crab does,
For you are soft inside and easily hurt.

C A N C E R

If someone speaks harshly to you,
tears spring to your eyes.
If a friend seems to prefer someone else,
you feel mortally wounded.
You brood over an insult
long after everyone else has forgotten.
Your friends may not even suspect you are
 hurt.
For instead of striking out in anger,
you retreat into your shell.
Others may coax, threaten or cajole,
but you will stubbornly maintain your injured
 silence,
and refuse to come out
till you feel safe again.

As the crab exists at the mercy of the waves
 and tides,
you are subject to the ebb and flow of your
 emotions.
You often respond emotionally rather than
 rationally,
and you reflect the emotions of others
as the moon reflects sunlight.
Your uncanny intuition lets you sense

C A N C E R

the way other people feel
even if they don't tell you.

The world often seems threatening
to a vulnerable creature like you.
So you prefer to stay
in a familiar corner of it.
You prefer old clothes, stories, furniture, and
 friends.
You hate to change and are happiest
when your life is regular and predictable.
A change of plans will be annoying to you.
A change of address will be traumatic.
Your home is very important to you,
for it's one place where you feel totally
 secure.
Changes in your home life will be threatening
 to you.

When things are going well,
you worry incessantly.
But your pessimism makes you stoical
in the face of misfortune.
You accept bad luck matter-of-factly

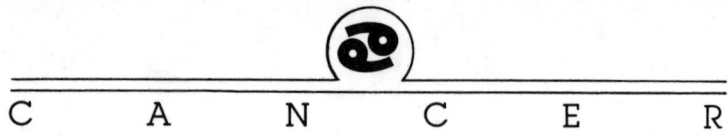

C　A　N　C　E　R

because you always expected it.
Instead of protesting your fate,
you wait patiently
for things to get better.

You seem so shy and quiet,
your friends may think
you'll do anything they want.
But Cancer is a sign of leadership.
You won't let yourself be pushed around.
You may not argue,
but you'll do things your own way.

C A N C E R

Beneath your cautious and practical exterior,
you are a dreamy romantic—a true moon child.
With your sensitivity
you may become a poet, a painter, or a musician.
But doubt may inhibit your creative potential.
You may submit your dreams
to the test of practicality
and never embark on romantic adventures.
Or you may worry about what people will think
And dream your dreams so secretely
That few people will guess
you dream at all.

C A N C E R

but you're probably not 100% cancer

Do you recognize yourself? If you were born between June 21 and July 23, you may share most of the personality traits typical of Cancer. But you probably feel that you don't share all of them. This is not too surprising.

Knowing that someone is a Cancer or a Gemini is similar to knowing that he or she is Japanese, Italian, or Egyptian. A person's nationality tells you something about what the person might look like and how he might think and act. Someone who is Irish might have black hair, a round face and freckles. Someone who is of Scottish descent might be thrifty.

Yet knowing a person's nationality won't tell you everything. Not all people of the same nationality share the same traits. To get a clearer picture of the person, you would have to find out about the person's age, sex, religion, favorite sport and hobbies.

C A N C E R

In the same way, a person's sun sign can provide some general information. But it cannot reveal all of the aspects of a personality. If an astrologer wanted to know more about a person, he or she would have to find out exactly when and where the person was born. Then the astrologer would calculate the exact position of the sun, the moon and the planets of our solar system in relation to the earth at the moment of the person's birth.

Astrologers believe that human beings are affected by the same energies that cause the sun, the moon and the planets to move in their orbits. They believe that a chart showing the position of these heavenly bodies at the moment of birth can be a kind of blueprint giving clues to a person's personality and potential.

But drawing up such a chart is no easy matter, since the earth, as well as the sun, moon and planets, are all constantly in motion. Because of this movement, even identical twins born only minutes apart will have slightly different birth charts, and two

C A N C E R

Cancerians whose birthdays are ten days apart can be very different indeed.

Interpreting a birth chart is even more complicated than constructing it. That's why many astrologers advise beginners to start their study of astrology by learning about sun signs. Since the sun affects life on the earth more than the other stars and the planets do, the sun sign is a very important factor in a birth chart. Remember that it's not the only factor.

One more word of caution: it takes approximately 29 days for the sun to move through each of the twelve zones or sun signs of the zodiac. But the exact time when the sun passes from one zone to the next varies from year to year, so the dates listed for any sun sign are only approximate.

If you were born on June 21 you might be either Cancer or Gemini, and if your birthday is July 23, your sun sign could be Cancer or Leo. In order to tell for sure which you are, you would have to consult an astrological reference book called an ephemeris. After making certain corrections depending on precisely where you were born, you would have to look up your exact

C A N C E R

time of birth in order to see whether the sun had changed signs by then.

If you were born at one of these turning points and don't have access to an ephemeris, try reading about both signs. See if you can tell which description fits you better.

Your sun sign can't tell you everything about yourself. But it can give some general characteristics. In reading about your sun sign you may come to know and understand yourself better.

your cancerian appearance

Your sun sign affects your physical appearance, as well as your personality. Just remember that there are other factors at work and that you probably won't look exactly like this typical Cancerian portrait.

C A N C E R

The typical Cancerian has:
- a thin, bony body structure
- broad shoulders
- either unusually large or unusually small hands and feet
- one of these two types of faces:

  a round, soft face
  wide mouth
  round eyes, which give this type of Cancerian a wide-eyed, wondering look.

  Or, a long, thin face
  lower jaw thrust out
  mouth pursed in a perpetual frown
  small eyes spaced wide apart
  eyebrows knit together
  forehead lined from worry.
  This type of Cancerian may scowl even when happy.

C A N C E R

what you might expect

Your sun sign also affects the way you think and act. As you read the following descriptions of how a Cancerian might act in certain situations, see if you can recognize yourself. But remember this is a hypothetical person. Don't look for a mirror image of yourself. You will probably only catch glimpses of the you you know.

school

If your sun sign is Cancer, you probably worry a lot about your school work, even though you don't need to. You're never sure whether you've learned something well enough. If your teacher assigns ten math problems, you may do another five, just to make sure you really understand. If you're assigned a chapter in your history book, you'll probably read it over

C A N C E R

twice. You will stay up late studying for a test and after you take it, you'll be sure you failed. But when you get your paper back, you'll find you got an A.

It's important for you to have a good relationship with your teacher. You are not the kind of student who is always waving your hand in the air, trying to get the teacher's attention. Instead, you are quiet and rather shy. You will probably choose to sit near the back of the room.

Even when you know the answer, you will probably stare down at your desk or out the window, rather than raise your hand. But you'll be hoping the teacher will notice you. You are eager for praise and attention, even though you don't actively seek it.

If your teacher is kind and understanding, you will gradually become more confident and will volunteer your ideas more often. You will listen carefully and hand in every assignment. You will study hard. If you don't understand something right away, you will work at it until you do. You may become one of the better students in the class.

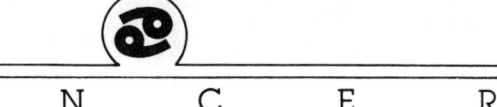

C A N C E R

But if your teacher ridicules you, you will be miserable and your school work will suffer. Cancerians are very sensitive and are easily wounded by criticism. If you get a math problem wrong and your teacher makes a sarcastic remark about it, you will feel like crawling under your desk. You'll feel as though you can't do anything right.

The entire class may have worked the problem wrong, and it may have been the teacher's fault for not explaining it properly. But that won't make you feel any better. You will be convinced that you are stupid and worthless. Instead of getting angry, you will merely feel despondent. It will take a lot of encouragement for you to regain your confidence.

Cancerian Helen Keller was lucky enough to have a patient and sympathetic teacher to encourage her. When Helen was very young, she contracted an illness which left her both blind and deaf. Because she could not hear, she lost her ability to speak. Nearly everyone thought it would be impossible for her to learn anything at all.

CANCER

But with the help of her teacher, Anne Sullivan, Helen Keller learned Braille and sign language. Eventually she even learned to speak again and to "hear" by feeling the vibrations in a person's throat. Helen Keller graduated from college with honors. She became a famous writer and lecturer. Her courage and determination inspired blind and deaf people everywhere.

The obstacles you encounter probably won't be as great as the ones Helen Keller faced. But if your sun sign is Cancer, you, too, may be able to accomplish astonishing feats if you get enough encouragement.

Once you decide to do something, you will work with single-minded determination. But it may take you a while to decide. Cancerians are not impulsive. You will rarely act without carefully calculating all the risks involved.

Perhaps you're considering running for the student council. You'll wait until the last moment to submit your name as a candidate because you'll want to assess the strength of your opponents. You'll calculate the number of votes you'll need and try to

C A N C E R

determine how many you might get. You won't run unless you feel you're almost sure to win.

If you decide you have a good chance, you'll organize an active campaign. You'll get your friends to put up posters in every available space and urge students to vote for you. On election day, you'll probably win your seat on the council hands down. And you'll be good at the job. Despite their quiet natures, Cancerians are basically leaders, not followers. They do well in positions of responsibility.

Cancerians are gentle and dreamy. But they are also practical and matter-of-fact. Some tend to be more one way than the other, but most are a curious combination of these contradictory qualities. That July-born entrepreneur who set up a concession stand at the football games last fall and sold a record number of hot dogs, probably writes lyric poetry in his spare time. And the dreamy Cancerian who sits at the lunch table, staring out the window and forgetting to eat, may be tallying up the receipts from her two paper routes and three babysitting jobs.

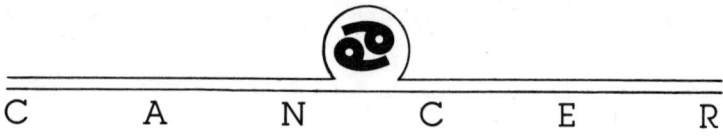

C A N C E R

If you are a Cancerian, you probably have a vivid imagination. When you're reading a story, you get totally involved. You're oblivious to everything that's going on around you. If you're reading something particularly exciting, you may not even hear the teacher dismiss the class. You'll read on, while the rest of the students put away their books and file out the door. Suddenly you'll notice that you're sitting in an empty room.

You're idealistic and romantic. You like reading myths and legends and stories about long-ago times when heroes accomplished mighty deeds despite great odds. You also like to read about the lives of modern heroes like President John Kennedy and Martin Luther King.

History comes alive for you because you can easily imagine that you were there. If your social studies class is studying the Civil War, you won't have trouble remembering what happened when. You'll be able to imagine yourself as a Confederate soldier defending his home and crops from General Sherman's army—and as a lonely Union

CANCER

drummer boy warming his hands by a campfire at Gettysburg.

Your memory for dates and events may be quite remarkable, but you probably have difficulty remembering math formulas. You're more interested in personal relationships than in parallel lines and triangles. So you probably won't find math as interesting as reading or social studies—unless you can see a way of actually putting it to use. You hate doing pages of multiplication problems, but you don't mind figuring out the interest on your savings account.

If your sun sign is Cancer, you are probably sensitive and emotional. But even people who know you well may not be able to guess how you're feeling at any moment. Cancerians don't shout and pound the table when they get angry. They don't jump up and down excitedly when they feel happy. They rarely talk about their fears. But many Cancerians are able to communicate their feelings indirectly through poetry, art, music, or drama.

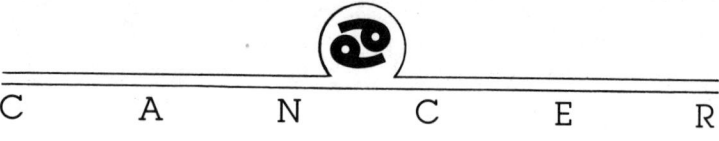

C A N C E R

If your sun sign is Cancer, you may be very talented in one of these areas. But you will probably be shy about performing in public. The sight of an auditorium full of people waiting to hear you sing a solo will make your stomach do flipflops. But if you are able to force yourself to walk out on the stage and forget about the people in the audience, you will undoubtedly give a very moving performance.

sports and hobbies

Cancerians do not pride themselves on their physical fitness. If your sun sign is Cancer, you probably don't boast about the number of push-ups you did before breakfast or the 3-miles you ran before school. If someone suggests playing a game of touch football or having a race around the block, you're likely to decline.

An occasional Cancerian, such as tennis star Arthur Ashe, will enjoy dashing about, but

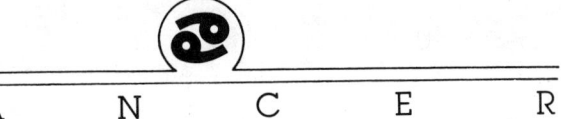

C A N C E R

most July people will choose quiter forms of recreation, such as a stroll through the park or a picnic in the woods. With their sensitive, poetic natures, Cancerians enjoy contemplating nature, and they prefer to do it at a leisurely pace. One Cancerian, Henry David Thoreau, enjoyed solitude so much that he spent two years living alone in a hut near Walden Pond.

You may not be able to spend two years in the woods, but if you are a typical Cancerian, you, too, will seek out stillness when the world seems too complicated and tumultuous. Possibly you will find yourself lost in thought beside some body of water. Cancer is a water sign, and most Cancerians find themselves inevitably drawn toward the beach or the seashore.

Maybe you'll sit, as Thoreau did, beside a quiet pond. Or perhaps you'll paddle a canoe down a lazy stream. Or you may enjoy watching the early morning mist rise from the lake as you're rowing to your favorite fishing spot. Maybe you'll hoist up your mainsail, tighten your jib and head your sailboat out to sea.

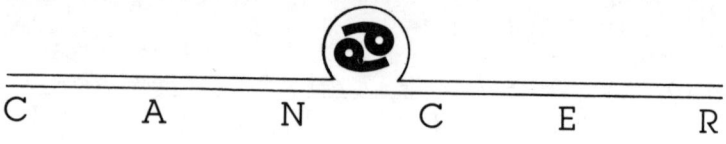

C A N C E R

You may enjoy swimming, water-skiing, or scuba diving. Or perhaps you like to dig in the sand for interesting rocks or shells. Cancerians tend to be avid collectors. If you don't collect rocks, you may save gum wrappers, marbles, or baseball cards. You probably collect all these things and a dozen others besides. You're likely to come home from a walk with a pile of rocks that might contain interesting fossils, a selection of colored autumn leaves, and a caterpillar constructing a cocoon around a twig. Your room tends to look like a section of the natural history museum.

money

Cancerians save money as enthusiastically as they save everything else. If your sun sign is Cancer, you probably have a couple of dollars hidden under your mattress, a dime tucked in your shoe, and a tidy sum stashed away in your piggy bank. It makes you feel secure to know

CANCER

you have some cash ready in case of emergency.

You like to count your money and figure out what you could buy. But you'll probably debate for a long time before you part with any of it. Not even rich Cancerians spend money freely. Cancerian John D. Rockefeller was a millionaire many times over—yet he gave his sons a small allowance and made them account for every penny. He felt himself to be the soul of generosity when he gave away dimes to small children.

If you're a Cancerian, you aren't likely to play the role of the big spender and buy your friends expensive gifts in order to impress them. Cancerians don't yearn to acquire money for power or prestige and they don't spend it flamboyantly. For Cancerians, money represents security, and even if they have a lot of money, they're always worried that it won't be enough.

If you're a Cancerian, you probably won't become as rich as John D. Rockefeller, but it's unlikely you'll ever be poor. You'll work hard, seldom take financial risks, and

C A N C E R

spend your money frugally. But while you'll never be accused of throwing money away, you won't be stingy. You may refuse to lend a classmate 50c, but you'll spend $10 on your mother's birthday present. You appreciate quality and don't mind spending more money to acquire something of real value. Even though you have to save for a long time, you'd rather spend $150 on a well-built 10-speed bike than get a $30 3-speed model from the discount store.

If you're a typical Cancerian, you've probably tried lots of different ways of earning money. You probably set up your first Kool-aid stand when you were 3 or 4. Now you probably mow lawns, shovel walks, and rake leaves. You're probably also much in demand as a babysitter because you enjoy young children and are good at caring for them. Cancer is a protective, nurturing sign, and both male and female Cancerians make excellent "mothers."

You may also earn money by taking care of the neighbors' pets when they're away. You have a gentle touch, and animals instinctively trust you. You are conscientious

C A N C E R

about caring for pets—either your own or the neighbors'. You never forget to feed the fish, let the cat out, or fill the dog's water dish.

Your protectiveness also extends to plants. If you have a garden, your tomatoes and cucumbers are probably the envy of the neighborhood. If you don't grow vegetables, you may care for a pot of geraniums in the kitchen. Or perhaps you keep an ivy or a spider plant in your room. Your plants will thrive because you are careful to water them just enough and to keep them where they get the right amount of light. People will tell you that you have a green thumb.

new things

The Cancerian collecting instinct leads July people to stockpile things. When they get ready to bake cookies and take a package of chocolate chips down from the shelf, they like to know they have four or five packages left in reserve. Cancerians don't consider this hoarding. To

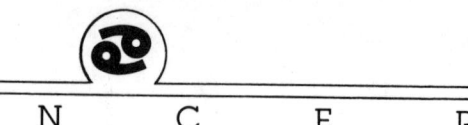

C A N C E R

them, it's being prepared. They have a horror of running out of anything.

It's difficult to buy presents for Cancerians. They are delighted to be remembered, but they like to save gifts, rather than use them. Your sister may notice that your wallet is ripped and buy you a new one for your birthday. You will thank her profusely, but two months later you'll take her to a movie and pull out your old, worn billfold to pay for the tickets. Your sister will be puzzled and hurt. She'll think you didn't like her present. But that won't be true. You are simply used to your old wallet—it has a familiar feel to it. You feel it would be a shame to throw it away. It gives you a great pleasure to have a new wallet, but you prefer to keep it in your drawer for a while.

Cancerians can't bear to throw anything away. They save birthday cards, old arithmetic papers, broken record players, leftover food, and bent nails. Their closets are full of clothes they never wear but couldn't part with.

Cancerians cling to traditions and familiar ways of doing things as tenaciously as

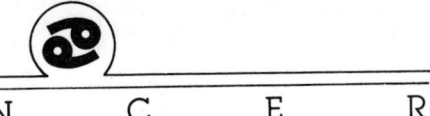

C A N C E R

they hang onto comfortable old tennis shoes. If your sun sign is Cancer, you tend to be suspicious of anything new. If you've always had turkey with chestnut stuffing for Thanksgiving and your mother decides to try roast goose with apples for a change, you'll object mildly. But if you've always spent the holiday at home and your father proposes spending a weekend at a ski resort instead, you may refuse to go.

Change is painful for you. The more drastic the change, the more you'll resist and the harder it will be for you to adjust. Moving is a possibility too dreadful for you to contemplate, as it would upset all your established routines. If your family moves to another city and you have to get used to a new house, a new school and new friends all at once, you'll feel as though your whole world has turned topsy turvy.

travel

Exotic names of far-away places hold little allure for the

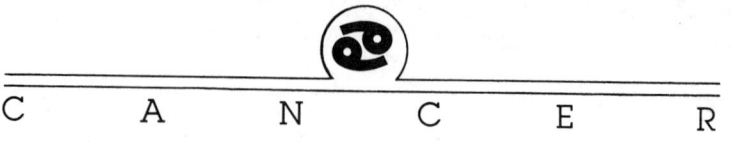

C A N C E R

Cancerian. You'll travel if you must, but you'd rather stay home. Of course Cancerians differ in what they consider "home territory." Writer Henry David Thoreau refused to budge from Concord, Massachusetts. Julius Caesar, on the other hand, explored the outer reaches of the known world, but that was because he'd decided to conquer the world for Rome.

Whether you are content to remain in your home town or are determined to acquire an empire, if you're a true Cancerian you'll want someplace to call your own. And once you are settled, you won't take kindly to being uprooted.

home and family

If your sun sign is Cancer, home is probably your favorite place to be. Your parents may worry because you're at home so much. They may try to get you involved in after-school sports activities, in a church group, in 4-H, or a Scout troop. But you insist on staying home. You can spend

CANCER

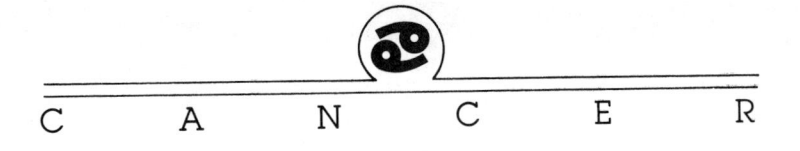

hours reading or listening to records all by yourself and be perfectly happy.

Sometimes you like to be with friends, but you prefer to have them come to your house. You are so attached to your family that you get lonesome spending the night at a friend's house or a week at summer camp.

You are happiest when your whole family is at home together. If your father has to travel a lot, you'll worry when he's gone. If your older sister goes away to college, you'll count the days until she comes home for vacation. You'll miss her more than your parents do.

You'll enjoy getting together with your grandparents and great-grandparents, aunts, uncles and cousins for holidays or family reunions. You aren't just being polite when you ask Great Aunt Sallie to tell you about baking bread on a wood-burning stove or riding to church in a horse-drawn sleigh—you're really interested. If Aunt Sallie gives you a silver teaspoon that was her mother's, you will treasure it and pass it on to your own children. You like the feeling of being tangibly connected with the past.

C A N C E R

friends

If you're a typical Cancerian, you aren't the kind of person who will strike up a conversation with a stranger. On a bus or plane, you will bury yourself in a book or magazine to avoid speaking to the person next to you. You hate big parties where you're supposed to circulate and make casual conversations—you can never think of anything to say.

Making new friends is a long and painful process for you. You are always wondering what other people think of you and are afraid you won't seem interesting—or clever—or attractive enough. You worry that your hair is too long—or too short; that you smile too much — or not enough; that you've said something that would offend someone. It's hard for you to realize that other people don't judge you nearly as harshly as you judge yourself.

It takes a long time for you to feel confident enough of another person's friendship to just relax and be yourself. That's

CANCER

why you value your few close friends so highly. There aren't many people besides members of your family with whom you feel completely at ease. You will be devoted to your close friends and willing to give them unlimited amounts of time and attention.

But you demand a lot from friends. You will be completely loyal to your friends and will expect absolute loyalty in return. You will never be completely sure that your friends like you as much as you like them. You will require constant reassurance.

Many people will be comfortable in the close kind of relationship you desire. They may feel smothered by your solicitous attention. You must try not to cling to the people you love or to require more of them than they're able to give.

health – Rx for cancer

Your tendency to bury your feelings inside you can cause problems with your sensitive stomach and digestive system. Your hidden worries can also cause

C A N C E R

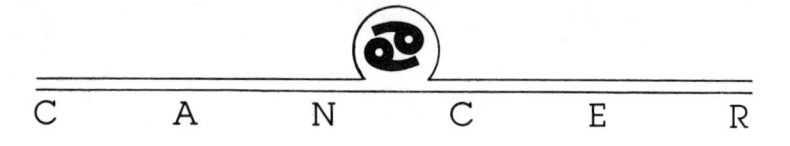

ulcers and other digestive problems. You must try to find acceptable means of expressing your feelings. Don't be afraid to yell if you get angry or to talk out your problems with a friend if you're afraid. Above all, make sure you get plenty of physical exercise, even though, if you are typically Cancerian, you don't particularly enjoy vigorous activity.

The state of your health will depend on how well you learn to control your emotions. If you cultivate a serene and optimistic disposition, you will hardly ever be sick. But if you succumb to fear and worry, your health will suffer. Cancerians feel their emotions so intensely that they can actually become physically ill from worry or sadness.

Your state of mind will also determine how fast you recover. When you are feeling cheerful, you'll be able to shake a cold in just a day or two, but if you get depressed, you may sniffle and cough for weeks.

You must try to curb your desire to seek sympathy when you are ill. Sympathy merely reinforces your tendencies toward self-pity and may actually prolong your illness.

C A N C E R

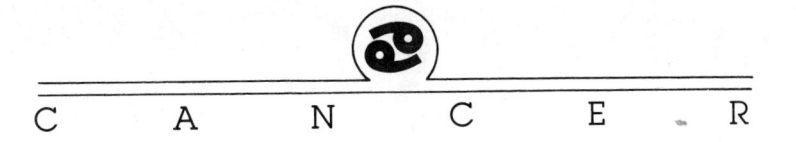

Instead, try to stay cheerful and optimistic. Your health will improve.

other cancerians like you

Some of your Cancerian tendencies will be more noticeable when you're young. Others will become apparent as you grow older. Some traits will be especially evident in certain roles or occupations. See if you can identify typical characteristics in other Cancerians you may know.

if your older sister is a cancerian

It was hard for her to leave home. Before she went away to

C A N C E R

college, she cried a lot. She was worried about moving into a dormitory with people she didn't know. She was afraid that work would be too hard, that she wouldn't like her roommate, and that no one would like her.

For the first few weeks after she started school, she called home every night. Your parents were afraid she would be too homesick to stay in college. In the end, she did, but your family's phone bills ran high for a few months.

When your sister came home for vacation, she always got upset if your mother had moved the living room furniture or bought a new rug. Your sister hates to have anything changed. When she comes home she wants everything to be as she remembered it.

Now your sister is married and lives in another city. But she still writes home every week, telephones frequently and comes home for holidays. She is the only one in the family who always remembers everyone's birthday.

C A N C E R

if your mother is a cancerian

She is probably an excellent cook. She doesn't like to use cake mixes or packets of instant soup—she makes her cakes and soups from scratch. She even bakes her own bread and cans fruit and tomatoes from her garden. When you come home from school and open the kitchen door, you can smell cookies baking or soup bubbling on the stove.

Your mother is always worring about your health. If you have a cough or a sniffle, she insists you stay home from school. She takes your temperature every hour and feeds you hot chicken broth.

Your friends usually get their own breakfasts, but your mother is always up before you are. By the time you stumble sleepily downstairs, she has orange juice and hot oatmeal waiting for you and she hovers over you until you finish it. In the winter you're never able to sneak out the door without

C A N C E R

wearing your boots and muffler. If it's raining, she'll insist on driving you to school.

Your mother always has a snack waiting for you when you come home from school. She's eager to hear how your day went. She asks you about the science test you worried over and how the teacher liked the story you wrote. If you're feeling discouraged, she'll cheer you up.

If you're playing a football game after school or performing in a concert, your mother will always be there, sitting in the front row. When you're out late at night, she'll always wait up for you. Sometimes you wish your mother wouldn't fuss over you so much—but most of the time you enjoy all the attention.

if your grandfather is a cancerian

He's a history buff. He can tell you about all the battles in World War

C A N C E R

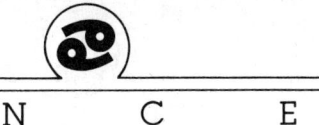

II and can show you the positions of the various armies. He collects old railroad schedules and can show you how a load of grain would have been routed from Chicago to Salt Lake City in 1899. You like to look at your grandfather's stamp collection. He has stamps from nearly every country in the world, including some rare old Russian stamps from the time of the revolution.

Once your grandfather made you a dollhouse that stood as high as your shoulders and looked like a Victorian mansion with turrets and gingerbread trim. Another time your grandfather made a model ship. But he didn't use a kit with pieces already cut out. He got the plans for a real sailing ship and cut all the pieces of wood exactly to scale.

Your grandfather rarely talks about himself—you never know how he's feeling or whether he's worried about something. He'd rather discuss his stamp collection or city politics. But if you ask about the faded old photographs he keeps on the mantle, he may tell you about his father, who came to the United States from Germany at the turn of the century and made a fortune in the dry

C A N C E R

goods business—and about his father's father, who was a shopkeeper in a small village in the old country.

Your grandfather speaks rather formally and precisely. Even on the hottest days, he wears a carefully starched long-sleeved shirt and a tie. He looks as though he were about to go somewhere, but he rarely leaves his apartment. He's interested in what's going on in the world, but he prefers to observe from a distance. He knows all about the children who play in the schoolyard next door, but he's too shy to go out and talk to them. He's interested in politics, but he'll watch a political debate on television rather than attend a party caucus. He even has his groceries delivered, rather than walking two blocks to the grocery store. He's perfectly content just staying home.

cancerian careers

If your sun sign is Cancer, you are probably an ideal

CANCER

employee. You are responsible and dependable. You always finish what you set out to do. Your boss will rarely find you chatting with a friend on the telephone or lingering at the water cooler when you're supposed to be working. You will do whatever you're asked to do, even if you find the work boring and repetitious. Even if you're not completely happy with your work, you will hesitate to leave and look for another position.

However, you won't be satisfied staying on the lower rungs of the ladder all your life. If you don't get regular raises and advance as quickly as you think you should, you will leave—however reluctantly—because you'll be aiming for the top. Most likely you'll get there, eventually. Cancerians nearly always accomplish what they set out to do.

You have a number of talents and interests which you should consider when choosing a career.

Your need to protect and care for others may lead you toward:

— teaching (especially small

CANCER

children)
- medicine — doctor, nurse,
- pharmacist
- social work

Your shrewdness and skill in managing money will make business an attractive field for you. Your excellent memory will help you keep track of small but important details. Your Cancerian urge to protect the interests of others can lead you into a number of business-related fields, such as:

- banking and finance
- accounting
- insurance
- hotel management

famous people born under the sign of cancer

Arthur Ashe, tennis player
John Quincy Adams, statesman
Louis Armstrong, musician
Ingmar Bergman, film producer

CANCER

Milton Berle, comedian
Julius Caesar, ruler
Marc Chagall, painter
Jean Cocteau, author
Calvin Coolidge, United States President
Bill Cosby, comedian
Phyllis Diller, comedienne
Stephen Foster, songwriter
John Glenn, astronaut
Oscar Hammerstein, musician
Ernest Hemingway, author
Henry VIII, ruler
Helen Keller, unique intellectual
Charles Laughton, actor
Gertrude Lawrence, singer
Anne Lindbergh, author
Marcel Proust, author
Freddie Pring, actor
Rembrandt, painter
John D. Rockefeller, wealthy businessman
Nelson Rockefeller, politician
Red Skelton, comedian
Ringo Starr, musician
Henry David Thoreau, author
Duke of Windsor, ruler
Andrew Wyeth, painter

sun signs for young people

creative education

ARIES	•	March 21 — April 20
TAURUS	•	April 20 — May 21
GEMINI	•	May 21 — June 21
CANCER	•	June 21 — July 23
LEO	•	July 23 — August 23
VIRGO	•	August 24 — September 23
LIBRA	•	September 23 — October 23
SCORPIO	•	October 23 — November 22
SAGITTARIUS	•	November 22 — December 22
CAPRICORN	•	December 22 — January 20
AQUARIUS	•	January 20 — February 18
PISCES	•	February 18 — March 20